Prisoner of
love

IBRAHIM OLAWALE

First published in Great Britain as a softback original in 2021

Copyright © Ibrahim Olawale

The moral right of this author has been asserted.

All rights reserved.

No part of this publication may be reproduced, stored in a retrieval system, or transmitted, in any form or by any means, without the prior permission in writing of the author, nor be otherwise circulated in any form of binding or cover other than that in which it is published and without a similar condition including this condition being imposed on the subsequent purchaser.

Design by Buzzdesignz

Published by The Roaring Lion Newcastle LTD.

ISBN: 978-1-913636-90-6

Email:
books@theroaringlionnewcastle.com

Website:

www.theroaringlionnewcastle.com

DEDICATION

To everyone who has escaped
from the prison of love

Table of Contents

Acknowledgements 1
Hopeless Romantic 3
Prisoner of Love 4
Heal the World 5
Our Love 6
True Love 7
Cheating Ex 8
My Body 9
The Woman of Your Dreams 10
Seeds of Love 11
Cobwebs 12
Love Castle 13
Flowery Words 14
Single and Winning 15
Say No More 16
Shadows from the Past 17
Sisterhood 18
Trapped 19
Immigrant's Tale 20
Bio 21
Author's Note 22

Acknowledgements

My profound gratitude goes to God for the grace through the journey and to my ever-supportive family for their endless love and encouragement.

My friends Abiodun Coker and Ademola Adeyemo, for their contribution and encouragement towards this project – you guys deserve a holiday to the moon. I do not take you for granted.

Sincere thanks to my editors, HungryBookstore and Adeola Juwon Gbalajobi. Thanks for the stellar work!

Worthy of mention is my writing mentor, Tolu' A. Akinyemi (Lion of Newcastle). Thank you for your total support of my foray into poetry and for holding me by the hand to ensure that I got off to a great start. A true African giant!

POEMS

Hopeless Romantic

I am a hopeless romantic;
my heart sings joyous melodies at the sight of you.

I am a hopeless romantic;
your love engulfs my heart to its depth.

I am a hopeless romantic;
my life is synced with yours, till death do us part.

Prisoner of Love

Release me from the prison of unrequited love;
let your heart be my sanctuary.

Release me from the prison of unrequited love;
let us embrace new beginnings.
my remembrance of you is sore like an open wound.

Release me from the prison of unrequited love;
let us be one again.

Heal the World

This is how we change the narrative –
sing a song of hope and
use your voice to heal the world.

The world wears turmoil like a dress;

distress lingers in the neighbourhood
and commotion is a ticking bomb.

Remember – your voice is the remedy
that will knit this broken world together.

Our Love

We lost our love the night we warred with words,
your words cutting through my heart like a hot
knife on butter.

Our love turned sour
that day your words thrust like a dagger within
my soul.

Our love went south
that morning I read your farewell note.

True Love

I drowned in the ocean of true love
when I loved blindly and you could do no wrong.

I was lost in the sea of true love
when our love capsized and I became a wreck.

I was killed on the altar of true love
when your darkened heart led me to death.
My tombstone was inscribed with the words:
He lived and died for love.

Cheating Ex

My ex was a skilled cheater.
Cheated the night after we took vows,
and kept a straight face.

My ex was a blatant liar;
lying was a favourite sport.

My ex was a serial cheater.
Cheated in and out of love
to satisfy unholy desires.

My ex was a serial killer.
Killed our growing love
and I shattered like a cracked egg.

My Body

I have learnt to love my body with its scars,
to treat it like a prized ornament,
to worship it and give it the care it deserves.
I have learnt to love myself.

The Woman of Your Dreams

Being the woman of your dreams is no prize to covet.

Man, I am not a trophy to be won –
I am a whole human with dreams and feelings too.

I am not a trophy to be won –
I'm more than an object to fulfil your fantasy.

Seeds of Love

Our love has lost its flavour
and sparkle.

The foundation of our love wasn't strong;
it was built on sinking sands,

and as hail and sandstorms threatened,
our love crashed like a sandcastle.

Cobwebs

Your love in my heart was once green like grass
until the weeds grew and thorns tore into our
flesh.

The mention of your name once filled me with
goosebumps
and butterflies before it became soured by hate.

Our home of love has been overtaken by
cobwebs;
all that's left are haunting memories.

Love Castle

This love castle is shaking like a house with no foundation.

Your words were poetry that serenaded my soul.

When you asked if I would be your sidekick,

I replied, *Why not.*

I built my castles in the air with a partner who was not my own.

Who said "I do" to a woman who calls him lover?

The day our love castle crashed, the bubbles clouding my eyes disappeared.

Flowery Words

Don't flatter me.
Don't use flowery words to sweep me off my feet,
then trash me into the land of the forgotten.
Don't hide your intentions behind sugar-coated words;
my heart is not to toy with.

Single and Winning

I'm single and happy,
flourishing with a spring in my step.

Tell them being single is not a curse,
a label for loneliness.

I'm single and happy,
content with myself.

The overbearing stigma of my status
won't weigh me down.
I'm single but not lonely;
I'm happy with my life.

Say No More

Bury this tale of woe;
exile it to the city of lost memories.
Say no more about this untrue love.

Your love is a shackle;
I'm trapped in a prison of emotion.

Free me from this web of your ~~love~~ lies,
it was choking me.

Shadows from the Past

We lost the virtue of serenity when our love tethered
and spiralled into a cloud of hate.

The shadows from the past were haunting
and overshadowed our blooming love.

Your voice quaked like a grinding axe
when the shadow of the past reared its ugly head.

Sisterhood

She burnt the bridge of sisterhood
for clout and *wokeness*.

Untruths became gospel
when the mudslinging swirled
into a ferocious whirlwind.

The cycle of falsehood was broken
when she was paid in her own coin.

Trapped

I said "I do" under the pressure of
joining the league of the married.
It's been three years in this prison of love.

Where I come from, divorce is a taboo.
They say he will change,
but only God can change a man.

My lean figure says it all.
I have fasted and prayed,
scheming for an escape from this prison of love.

Immigrant's Tale

When my land turned yellow with drought,
I went in search of greener pastures,
wading through turbulent seas and battering
storms.

An immigrant's story is a tale of sorrow;
his face tells of his longing for home.
But when home loses its virtue,
a man becomes a fugitive in a foreign land.

Bio

Ibrahim is a poet and creative writer. He is a graduate of International Business Management and works as a Cyber Security consultant. He hails from Lagos, Nigeria and believes in the power of words and its effects. When not writing, you can find him watching football and listening to music.

Author's Note

Thank you for the time you have taken to read this book. I hope you enjoyed the poems in it.

If you loved the book and have a minute to spare, I would appreciate a short review on the page or site where you bought it. I greatly appreciate your help in promoting my work. Reviews from readers like you make a huge difference in helping new readers choose a book.

                    Thank you!
                Ibrahim Olawale

www.ingramcontent.com/pod-product-compliance
Lightning Source LLC
Chambersburg PA
CBHW021455080526
44588CB00009B/861